BITES AND STINGS

ELAINE LANDAU

Marshall Cavendish Benchmark
99 White Plains Road
Tarrytown, New York 10591
www.marshallcavendish.us

Expert Reader: Leslie L. Barton, M.D., professor of Pediatrics, University of Arizona College of Medicine, Tucson, Arizona

Library of Congress Cataloging-in-Publication Data
Landau, Elaine.
    Bites and stings / by Elaine Landau.
        p. cm. — (Head-to-toe health)
    Summary: "Provides basic information about bites and stings and their prevention"—Provided by publisher.
    Includes bibliographical references and index.
    ISBN 978-0-7614-2850-3
1. Bites and stings—Juvenile literature. I. Title.

RD96.2.L36 2009
617.1—dc22
2007043022

Editor: Christine Florie
Publisher: Michelle Bisson
Art Director: Anahid Hamparian
Series Designer: Alex Ferrari

Photo research by Connie Gardner

Cover photo by Rick Barrantine/RF/CORBIS

The photographs in this book are used by permission and through the courtesy of:
Photo Researchers: Phanie, 4; Jeremy Burgess, 16; Scott Camazine, 17; Super Stock: Pacific Stock, 6; age footstock, 7; Geri Lavrov, 15; Lisette Le Bon, 23; Getty Images: Lori Adamski Peek, 8; Digital Rail Road: Solvin Zank/drr.net, 9; PhotoEdit: Richard Hutchings, 10; Michael Newman, 11, 21; Jonathan Nourok, 12; Jeff Greenberg, 19; Corbis: Joe McDonald, 25.

Printed in China
1 3 5 6 4 2

CONTENTS

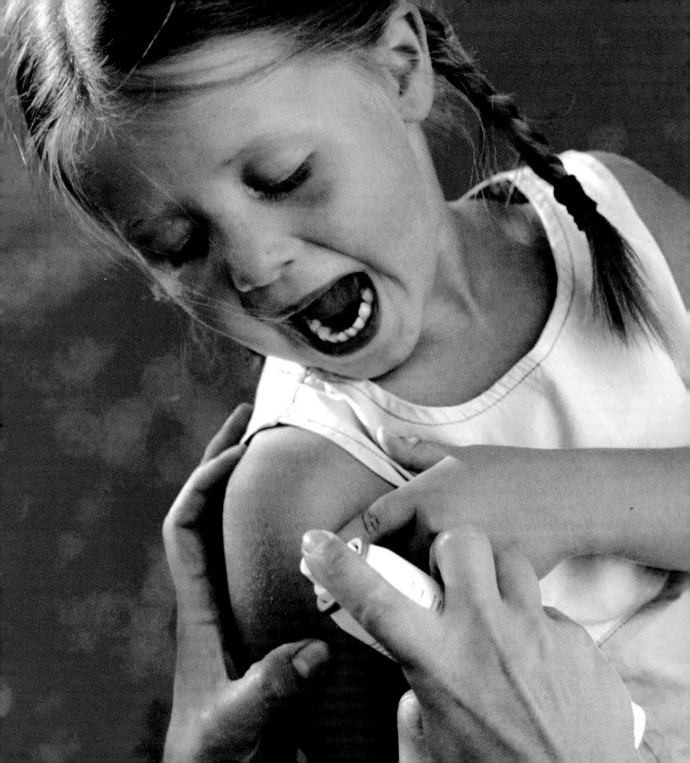

I'VE BEEN BITTEN!

Ouch! It bit me! Have you ever said this? Most people have been bitten or stung by some insect or animal at one time or another. Often you don't feel it happening. Later, your leg begins to itch. You look down and see a small reddish bump. It's a mosquito bite!

Other bites are harder to miss. Every year dogs bite about 4.7 million people. Over half are children. You know when that happens for sure!

You also would not miss being bitten by an alligator or shark. While these bites don't occur often—they have happened. In a number of cases those injured were kids.

WHY IT HAPPENS

Sometimes insects and animals bite out of fear. Bees, wasps, scorpions, and hornets sting when they sense danger.

◄ Insect bites can be itchy and annoying. Sprays and lotions can relieve the irritation they cause.

DON'T BECOME A SHARK-ATTACK SNACK!

Sharks do not view people as dinner. These meat-eating fish don't even find humans very tasty. Yet sometimes sharks attack swimmers. They mistake them for **prey** or food they usually eat. Here are some helpful hints to avoid a shark bite.

Don't swim in the ocean at dawn or dusk. That's feeding time for sharks. Also, be sure to stay out of the water if you have a cut. Sharks can smell blood for miles. It's not a good idea to wear shiny jewelry when swimming, either. Sharks can mistake it for fish scales.

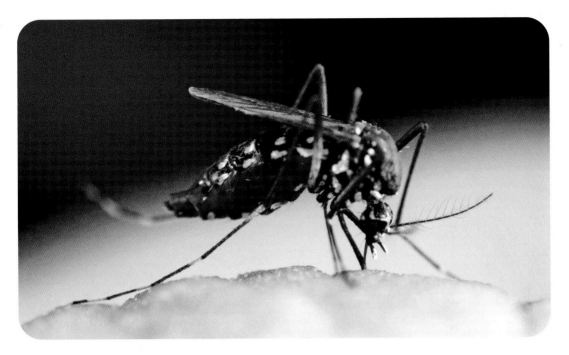

This mosquito is feeding on blood as it bites its host.

They may be protecting their area or nest. At times biting or stinging may be the only way they have to defend themselves.

Other times insects bite to live. Fleas and ticks feed on blood. Female mosquitoes need blood to lay eggs.

This is a book about bites and stings, how you can avoid them, and what to do if they happen anyway.

ITSY BITSY BITES

Hiking can be fun. To avoid bug bites, stay clear of tall grass and low-growing plants.

Don't let their tiny size fool you. Some very small insects and animals bite. Among the small biters are mosquitoes, gnats, fleas, and ticks.

STAYING BITE FREE

Nobody likes to be bitten. Sometimes it can't be helped. But you can try to make it happen less often.

When hiking, walk in the middle of the path. More insects are in the grass and brush along the sides. Play on well-mowed areas. High-growing grass is often home to lots of insects. Steer clear of marshy woodlands as well.

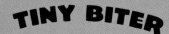

TINY BITER

Yuck, there's a tick on me!

Which of these is the best way to remove it?

a. Just pull the thing off you.

b. Only a doctor should remove a tick.

c. Grasp the tick with tweezers as close as possible to your skin.

Gently pull it off. Be sure to get the whole tick. Don't leave its head behind.

The correct answer is c.

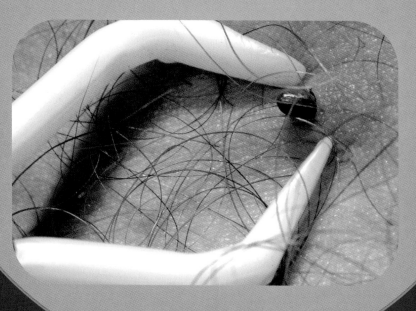

When outdoors, avoid getting bitten by wearing long pants and long-sleeve shirts.

DRESS FOR SUCCESS

Success in avoiding insect bites, that is. Wear long-sleeve shirts and long pants. Also, wear socks and shoes that are closed at the toe, not sandals. When hiking, some people tuck their pants into their socks and boots. This offers even more protection.

Also, try to choose light-colored clothing. It is easier to spot ticks and other insects on light colors.

ARE INSECT BITES DANGEROUS OR JUST ANNOYING?

Usually, insect bites are just annoying. But at times insects can carry diseases. Mosquitoes have been known to carry West Nile virus. Ticks can carry Lyme disease and Rocky Mountain spotted fever.

GO AWAY—DON'T COME BACK ANOTHER DAY

Insect repellants are also helpful in keeping away these small, unwanted visitors. However, insect repellants should be used with care. If possible, have an adult help you apply them.

Never spray an insect repellant over a cut, **wound**, or rash. Insect repellants should also be washed off when you come indoors. Use soap and water on the skin area that you sprayed. Some people take a bath instead. That does the job as well.

Insect repellants help keep pests away. Try to have an adult help you.

To help soothe itchy, bitten skin, spread calamine lotion on to the affected area.

Was the insect repellant sprayed on your clothing, too? If so, make sure those items are washed. Don't wear them again until they are.

In addition, remember to check yourself for ticks when you come in from the outdoors. This is especially important if you've been hiking in a wooded area or playing in high grass.

WHAT IF YOU ARE BITTEN ANYWAY?

Wash the bitten area with soap and water. If it hurts or itches, an ice pack may help. Applying a cold, wet cloth to the area can be useful, too. If there are many bites, try taking a cool bath. This is often soothing.

Some people find that **calamine lotion** stops the itching. Try keeping the calamine lotion in the refrigerator. The cool lotion often does the trick. There are also some good creams sold at drug stores. You should feel better soon. However, if a bite is very painful or swells a lot, you may need to see your doctor.

Try not to scratch the bite. Your fingers can have germs on them. This can lead to an infection. It's best to keep your nails short.

THE BUZZ ON BEE STINGS

Have you ever been stung by a bee? If you have, you know that it hurts. You probably don't want it to happen ever again.

Usually honeybees do not attack without cause. They sting to defend themselves. So you don't want to frighten them. You also don't want to draw them to you!

DID YOU KNOW?

A honeybee only stings once. When it stings, it dies.

AVOID BEING STUNG

Bees are drawn to flowers. So do your best not to look or smell like one. When spending time outdoors, don't wear perfume. Pass on using nice-smelling lotion, perfumed soap, or shampoo that day, too.

Don't let a bee think you are a sweet smelling flower. When outdoors, don't wear perfumes or use nice smelling shampoo.

Choose your clothes wisely for outings. Avoid brightly colored outfits, as most flowers are colorful. You also don't want to wear a flowered print to a picnic in the park.

Remember to bring a hat. Any type will do as long as it doesn't have flowers on it. The idea is to cover your hair.

When a bee sees a head of hair, it can mistake it for a furry animal. Furry animals sometimes steal honey from bees. So a bee is more likely to sting you when your head isn't covered.

Also try not to leave open cans of soda around when you're outdoors. Bees often fly into these. When you lift them to take a drink, look out. A scared bee may fly out and sting you.

A honeybee leaves its stinger behind after stinging a human finger.

WHAT IF YOU'RE STUNG ANYWAY?

When a bee stings it nearly always leaves its stinger behind. When this happens it also leaves its **venom** sac. The stinger continues to pump venom into your body. So it's important to remove the stinger right away.

If you are with an adult, ask that person to help you. A stinger can be removed easily when it's

BEWARE OF KILLER BEES!

Killer bees are not like common honeybees. These bees are extremely **aggressive**. They attack in large groups. At times hundreds of these bees take part in attacks. Killer bees do not give up easily, either. They have been known to chase people for up to a quarter of a mile. Luckily, killer bees tend to be fairly rare in the United States.

scraped out with a blunt-edged object. Often a credit card or dull knife works well.

Once the stinger is out, wash the area with soap and water. Try applying a cold pack to the stung area. If you don't have a cold pack, apply a cold, wet cloth instead.

If there is itching or pain, be sure to tell the adult who is taking care of you. There are some lotions available to soothe the itching. Often over-the-counter medicine can help with the pain.

WHEN BOWSER BITES

They may look cute and friendly, but to avoid being bitten, stay away from unfamiliar dogs.

Don't pet that dog! You don't know its owner. You don't even know where it came from. Yet it's so cute. You decide to take a chance.

That was your mistake. Suddenly the dog turns its head and snaps at you. Seconds later, it sinks its teeth into your hand. You can't remember anything that hurt this much.

What if this, or something like it, happened to you? Nearly half of all children under age twelve have been bitten by a dog. Would you know what to do?

First, tell the adult taking care of you. If there is no adult around, follow the steps below. Then get a responsible adult to help you as soon as you can.

DON'T PANIC

If the animal bite or scratch is bleeding, find a clean towel. Put this over the wound and press on it. This will help stop the bleeding.

Next, place the hurt area under a running faucet for at least five minutes. Gently wash the wound with soap and water. Carefully dry it and place a clean bandage over it.

THERE IS MORE TO DO

You will probably need to see your doctor. Sometimes an **antibiotic** is needed. This medicine stops the bite or scratch from becoming infected.

The doctor will also check and see if your tetanus shots are up to date. A tetanus shot protects you from the germs that cause the disease tetanus. These germs can enter your body from a break in your skin caused by an animal bite.

If possible, the animal that bit you should be found, too. The doctor needs to know if the animal (dog or cat) has had

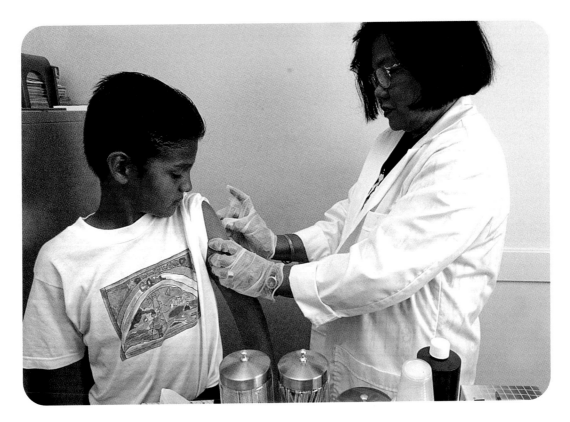

A tetanus shot may be given after a dog or cat bite to ward off bad germs.

its **rabies** shot. Rabies is a serious disease that can be given to humans by an infected animal.

Do not try to find the animal yourself. Don't send any of your friends to do this, either. An **animal control officer** should look for the animal.

What if an aggressive dog comes your way? Would you know what to do?

Don't scream or run away. Instead, pretend you are a statue and try to stand perfectly still. Do not look the dog in the eye. Dogs see this as aggressive behavior.

If the dog knocks you down, curl into a ball. This will help protect you. Keep your hands over your ears and stay as still as possible. Do not yell or try to roll away. Often the dog will lose interest and leave.

KNOW HOW TO ACT AROUND ANIMALS

Often you can avoid being bitten or scratched. Try following these helpful hints.

Never touch or pet an animal you don't know. This is especially important with dogs that are chained in yards or kept behind fences.

Don't think that puppies are always safe to pet. A teething puppy will chew on anything that comes its way. Make sure this is not your hand or finger.

Never tease or loudly scream at an animal. Remember, animals aren't humans. They don't know when you are playing.

It is never okay to throw marbles, stones, or anything else at an animal.

When with animals, behave properly to avoid being scratched or bitten.

Waving your arms or a stick in front of an animal is a bad idea as well. Never pull any animal's ears or tail.

More children go to emergency rooms for dog bites than for playground accidents. Don't be one of them. Act wisely around animals and treat them with respect. Know when it is smart to keep your distance.

In the Wild

Do you like hiking or camping? Adventures in the wild can be great! But remember that the wild is home to all sorts of animals.

ARE THERE SNAKES AROUND HERE?

About 2,700 different kinds of snakes exist in the world. However, only about 15 percent of these are poisonous. The poisonous ones in the United States include rattlesnakes, coral snakes, copperheads, and cottonmouths.

The best way to stay safe around these snakes is to stay as far away from them as you can. Don't try to trap a poisonous snake to get a closer look at it. Don't try to kill it, either.

Wear long pants and boots on outings in areas where there are snakes. This helps protect your ankles and feet from snakebites. If you are camping out, check your footwear every morning, where snakes and scorpions can sometimes rest. That kind of surprise is just no fun!

Some snakes bite. Avoiding them is the best way to prevent a bite.

WHAT IF YOU ARE BITTEN BY A POISONOUS SNAKE?

Snakebites are serious. If you are bitten, tell a responsible adult right away. You will need to get to an emergency room as soon as possible. Don't move about much. That helps spread the snake's venom through your body. Also, keep the bite spot lower than your heart.

NOT GREAT PETS

Wild animals do not make good pets. They should be left in the wild. Do not take a wild animal home hoping to tame it.

Raccoons look cute but can really bite and scratch. A baby alligator is also not a suitable pet. Never leave food out for an alligator. Do not try to touch one even if it seems sound asleep.

There's a lot to do outdoors. You should enjoy it all. You can safely share the outdoors with insects and animals that live there. With just a little extra care, you'll be more likely to avoid bites and stings as well!

GLOSSARY

aggressive — behaving in a fierce or threatening way

animal control officer — a person who works on incidents involving problems with animals

antibiotics — drugs used in treating various infections

antivenin — a medicine used to treat poisonous snakebites

calamine lotion — a lotion used to soothe itching or some mild skin rashes

insect repellant — a chemical substance used to keep insects away

prey — an animal hunted by another animal for food

rabies — a serious illness attacking the brain and spinal cord

venom — poison

wound — an injury in which the skin has been cut

FIND OUT MORE

BOOKS

Healy, Nick. *The World's Most Dangerous Bugs.* Mankato, MN: Capstone Press, 2006.

Landau, Elaine. *Sinister Snakes.* Berkeley Heights, NJ: Enslow Publishers, 2003.

Royston, Angela. *Stings and Bites.* Chicago: Heinemann Library, 2004.

Siy, Alexandra. *Mosquito Bite.* Watertown, MA: Charlesbridge, 2005.

Weber, Rebecca. *First Aid for You.* Minneapolis: Compass Point, 2004.

WEB SITES

Dogs & Kids

www.dogsandkids.ca

Visit this Web site to learn why dogs bite. There's also lots of information on how to protect yourself.

Twenty Reasons Not to Have a Pet Raccoon

www.isleauhaut.net/maskd/index.htm

Check out this Web site to learn why wild animals, like raccoons, should live in the wild.

Healthy Pets, Healthy People

www.cdc.gov/healthypets/

This Web site offers good information on how you can enjoy animals and still stay healthy.

INDEX

Page numbers in **boldface** are illustrations

ABOUT THE AUTHOR

Award-winning author Elaine Landau has written over three hundred books for young readers. Many of these are on health and science topics.

Ms. Landau received her bachelor's degree in English and Journalism from New York University and a master's degree in Library and Information Science from Pratt Institute. You can visit Elaine Landau at her Web site: www.elainelandau.com.